THE WITCH'S COOKBOOK

50 Wickedly Delicious Witchcraft-Inspired Recipes

FORTUNA NOIR

ROCK
POINT

CONTENTS

A Magical Hearth and Home

As the kitchen (or hearth) is the center of the home, magical energies are naturally drawn toward it. Let the magic of meals conjured in your kitchen spread love and sustenance beyond the walls of your abode. When we can share our good fortune (no matter how much or how little), our bounty grows threefold. Fuel those energies by encircling yourself with crystals and stones while you cook, but also celebrate the empty spaces and stillness. Use equipment you adore in order to infuse love and care into your cooking. And above all, cook and drink with a grateful heart.

With a mindful heart I honor Earth.
Her bounty never ends.

And blessed be, we share this meal
with family and with friends.

The foods we eat, the wine we share,
clean water that we have,

Are gifts bestowed, for much we owe,
which multiply when shared.

Sun Salutations

BREAKFAST AND BRUNCH

HAM AND GRUYÈRE QUICHE PLANETS

The planets play an important role in our lives. Their activity is believed to affect what we experience here on Earth. Use these quiches to celebrate the entire solar system, or customize them to your liking and enrich yourself with their properties.

Makes 16 quiches

INGREDIENTS

Flour, for dusting

1 (7 ounces, or 198 g) refrigerated piecrust

2 large eggs

½ cup (120 ml) whole milk

¼ teaspoon kosher salt

¼ teaspoon freshly ground black pepper

Fresh planetary vegetables and herbs, to garnish or include (optional)
  Dill for Mercury
  Thyme for Venus
  Allspice for Mars
  Nutmeg for Jupiter
  Chives for Saturn
  Carrot for Uranus
  Hemp hearts for Neptune
  Mushrooms for Pluto

⅓ cup (40 g) finely grated Gruyère cheese

2 slices cooked ham, chopped

TO PREPARE

1. Preheat the oven to 350°F (180°C).

2. Flour your work surface and a rolling pin. Roll out the piecrust to 12 inches (30 cm) in diameter and about the thickness of a coin.

3. Stamp out sixteen rounds from the dough with a 2½- to 3-inch (6.5 to 7.5 cm) scalloped cookie cutter. Press each round into the holes of a 24-cup silicone mini muffin pan (you can also use a greased regular mini muffin pan).

4. In a medium bowl, whisk together the eggs, milk, salt, black pepper, and the corresponding planetary herb, if incorporating rather than using as garnish. Spoon 1 tablespoon of the mixture into each pastry shell and sprinkle with the cheese and ham.

5. Bake until puffed and just set in the center, 20 to 25 minutes. Let cool to room temperature.

6. Arrange the quiche on a medium serving board. Garnish with the herbs (if using).

EARTHY BUCKWHEAT CREPES

In witchcraft, the elements are important, each having its own properties. Buckwheat, as an herb of the Earth, has several Earthlike qualities, such as the ability to attract wealth. As you eat these crepes, concentrate on what kind of wealth you'd like to attain.

Makes 8 crepes

INGREDIENTS

½ cup (60 g) all-purpose flour

½ cup (60 g) buckwheat flour

¼ teaspoon baking soda

¼ teaspoon kosher salt

3 large eggs

1½ cups (350 ml) milk

2 tablespoons unsalted butter, melted and cooled, plus extra for the pan

TO PREPARE

1. Place the flours, baking soda, and salt in a blender and pulse to combine. Imagine the dry ingredients coming together and harmonizing into exactly what you need.

2. Add the eggs, milk, and melted butter. Blend for 30 seconds. Let the batter rest for at least 1 hour, or up to 24 hours in the refrigerator. During this time, you can conceptualize what kind of wealth you want and how to get it.

3. Heat a 10- or 11-inch (25 or 28 cm) crepe pan or nonstick skillet over medium heat and brush with butter.

4. Once the skillet is hot, pour ⅓ cup (53 g) of the batter into the center of the pan. Tilt and swirl the pan so that the batter covers the surface. Cook until the underside is golden, 1 to 2 minutes, then flip as soon as the bottom is set. Cook for another 30 seconds. Transfer to a large plate and repeat with the remaining batter.

NJORD'S LOX AND BAGELS

Lox and bagels, a widely popular dish, has its roots in Scandinavia, where fishermen perfected the preparation of the briny salmon thousands of years ago. Njord (a.k.a. Njörðr), Scandinavian god of the sea, guided these men through rough seas and helped them with their catch. Thanks to him, we have this delicious meal with us today.

Serves 4 • Use a 13 × 20-inch (33 × 51 cm) board

INGREDIENTS

1 lemon, sliced into thin rounds

8 bagels of your choice

16 ounces (483 g) plain cream cheese

½ cup (70 g) capers, drained and rinsed

1 small red onion, thinly sliced

1 large heirloom tomato, sliced

1 hothouse cucumber, thinly sliced

12 ounces (340 g) lox or smoked salmon, thinly sliced

2 radishes, very thinly sliced

Fresh herbs, to garnish

Salt and freshly ground black pepper, to serve (optional)

TO PREPARE

1. Layer the lemon slices in a diagonal across the center of the board. Place the bagels around the edges of the board and on a plate to the side. Slice them for quick and easy topping.

2. Put the cream cheese and capers in serving bowls and anchor them at the top and bottom corners of the board.

3. Place the onion, tomato, and cucumber slices on the bottom half of the board.

4. Add the lox on a diagonal above the lemon slices and place the radishes on a diagonal above the lox. As you set this out, give thanks to Njord and the people who made this dish possible.

5. Fill in any gaps with the fresh herbs.

6. Serve with the salt and pepper (if using).

AUROCHS RUNE BREAKFAST SANDWICHES

Runes are symbols that help attract energies to you. Aurochs ᚢ (a.k.a. Uruz) is the rune of physical strength and vitality. Carving a rune on something gives that object the corresponding power. For these breakfast sandwiches, add the rune to either the bacon or the bread for an extra dose of magic to your meal.

Serves 4

INGREDIENTS

2 teaspoons olive oil

8 slices Canadian bacon

Cooking spray, for the pan

4 large eggs

Kosher salt

4 English muffins

4 slices cheddar cheese

TO PREPARE

1. Heat the oil in a large nonstick skillet over medium heat. Cook the Canadian bacon until crisp, 3 to 4 minutes per side. Carve ᚢ onto the bacon. Transfer to a plate.

2. Return the pan to the heat. Spray four Mason jar lid rings (or egg rings) with cooking spray and place flat sides down in the skillet.

3. Crack an egg into each ring, sprinkle with a pinch of salt, and break the yolk by stabbing it with a fork.

4. Pour hot water into the pan, halfway up the sides of the lid rings. Cover and cook until the eggs are set, about 2 minutes.

5. Meanwhile, split the English muffins and toast them. Place the bottom half of each English muffin on a serving board and top each one with a slice of cheese, melting it if you like, and two slices of Canadian bacon.

6. Use a slotted spatula to remove the eggs from the water. Unmold the eggs and place on the muffins. Top with the English muffin tops.

7. Serve immediately.

LAMMAS BREAKFAST FEAST

Lammas occurs in the summer on August 1 or 2. This holy day is about celebrating the harvest and the fruits of our labor. During this holiday, celebrate the gods and goddesses of prosperity and abundance with this egg, meat, and berry spread.

Serves 6 to 8 • Use a 6 × 18-inch (15 × 46 cm) board

INGREDIENTS

2 cups (300 g) mixed raspberries and blueberries

1 package (8 ounces, or 227 g) bacon, cooked

12 large eggs, scrambled

16 ounces (453 g) cream cheese, softened

8 bagels or sliced bread of your choice

Fresh herbs, to garnish

TO PREPARE

1. Put the mixed berries in a bowl, setting a few berries aside for garnish later. Set the bowl to the side of the board.

2. Place a piece of parchment paper on one end of the board and place the bacon slices on top.

3. Spoon the scrambled eggs into a warm 6-inch (15 cm) cast-iron skillet and place at the opposite end of the board to the bacon.

4. Transfer the cream cheese to a bowl and place on the side of the board.

5. Beside the board, pile up bread slices and the bagels. Slice them for quick and easy topping.

6. Fill any gaps with the fresh herbs and reserved berries.

CERRIDWEN GODDESS PANCAKES

In kitchen witchery, there are gods and goddesses of hearth and home. Cerridwen is the Welsh goddess of cauldrons, where spells and recipes come to life. As a home goddess, Cerridwen accepts wheat and milk as offerings, and the rest is up to you. As you make your pancakes, leave one for Cerridwen as a tribute.

Makes 12 of each pancake

INGREDIENTS

BUTTERMILK PANCAKES

2 cups (235 g) all-purpose flour

2 teaspoons sugar

1 teaspoon baking soda

Pinch of salt

2 large eggs

1¼ cups (300 ml) buttermilk

Butter, for the skillet

CINNAMON SUGAR PANCAKES

2 teaspoons sugar

1 teaspoon ground cinnamon

CHOCOLATE CHIP PANCAKES

6 teaspoons mini chocolate chips

TO PREPARE

1. To make the buttermilk pancakes: In a large bowl, whisk together the flour, sugar, baking soda, and salt. Add the eggs and buttermilk, and whisk until a smooth batter forms.

2. To make the cinnamon sugar pancakes: Transfer 1 cup (120 g) of batter to a second bowl and whisk in the sugar and ground cinnamon. Set aside.

3. Heat a griddle or nonstick skillet over medium-low heat. Once hot, brush with butter, then drop the plain buttermilk batter, 1 tablespoon per pancake, into the skillet, at least 2 inches (5 cm) apart. Cook until bubbly and starting to turn golden on the underside, about 3 minutes, then flip and cook for another minute. Cook 12 pancakes, adding butter as needed to the pan.

4. To make the chocolate chip pancakes: Using the remaining plain buttermilk batter, repeat the cooking instructions in step 3, sprinkling each pancake with ½ teaspoon mini chocolate chips as soon as the batter is poured onto the skillet.

5. Using the cinnamon sugar batter you set aside, repeat the cooking instructions in step 3.

6. Pile up and serve while hot.

GOLD PENTACLE PANCAKES

A witch's twist on silver dollar pancakes, these mini pentacle pancakes take their name from the Pentacle suit of tarot card decks. This suit represents finances, career choices, and material possessions. For extra guidance, have these pancakes for breakfast before making any important fiscal decisions.

Serves 4 to 6 • Use a 6 × 16-inch (15 × 41 cm) board

INGREDIENTS

1 recipe Cerridwen Goddess Pancakes (page 18)

Maple syrup, to serve

Butter pats, to serve

Chocolate chips, to serve

Mixed raspberries, blackberries, blueberries, and strawberries, to serve

Whipped cream, to serve (not pictured)

TO PREPARE

1. Place stacks of the pancakes down the center of the board and label them with toothpick flags.

2. Fill a small pitcher with maple syrup and place at the top of the board.

3. Fill in any gaps with the butter pats, chocolate chips, and berries.

4. Serve with the whipped cream.

Witch Tip

Carve light pentagrams on the pancakes for authenticity!

SUMMER SOLSTICE FRUIT MEDLEY

The summer solstice is the time when the Sun hangs the longest in the sky. It's the peak of the year, and during that peak, it's good to eat of the Earth's yield when she's at her best. Use honey's solar magic to enrich and bless this nutritious breakfast.

Serves 2 to 4 • Use a 12-inch (30 cm) round tray

INGREDIENTS

2 cups (430 g) yogurt of your choice

1 cup (150 g) blueberries

2 cups (300 g) granola of your choice

¼ cup (56 g) mixed sunflower seeds and pepitas

8 whole or shelled walnuts, chopped, plus more whole walnuts to garnish

¼ cup (85 g) honey

1 navel orange, sliced

1 kiwifruit, halved and segmented

8 ounces (227 g) strawberries, half sliced

1 green apple, sliced into wedges

1 cup (125 g) raspberries

1 pomegranate, segmented

TO PREPARE

1. Fill vessels with the yogurt, blueberries, granola, seeds, walnuts, and honey. Place the bowls of seeds, walnuts, and honey along the upper-right side of the tray. Place the bowl of blueberries in the upper left with the granola bowl placed on the diagonal below it. Set the bowl of yogurt to the side of the tray.

2. Shingle the orange slices along the left side of the tray.

3. Place the kiwi halves in the center of the tray and surround them with the strawberries, apple slices, raspberries, and pomegranate.

4. Fill in any gaps with whole walnuts.

5. Serve in bowls or layer up in jars to take with you. As you pour honey over the fruit, granola, or yogurt, say, "I thank the Sun and the Earth for this bounty."

LOVE, SHAKSHUKA

Shakshuka is an interesting dish. It was created after tomatoes were introduced into the Maghreb centuries ago. Its components carry the powers of protection and purification, and the main ingredient—tomato—represents love. When cooking for others, it's always good to include love, and this Arabian breakfast can help you do just that.

Serves 4 • Use a large skillet

INGREDIENTS

2 tablespoons olive oil

2 tablespoons harissa

1 medium onion, diced

1 red bell pepper, seeded and diced

4 cloves garlic, finely chopped

½ teaspoon kosher salt

1 teaspoon ground cumin

1 can (28 ounces, or 794 g) whole peeled tomatoes

4 large eggs

Chopped cilantro, to garnish

Bread of choice, to serve

TO PREPARE

1. Heat the oil in a large skillet over medium heat. Add the harissa, onion, pepper, garlic, salt, and cumin. Cook, stirring occasionally, until the onion and pepper have softened, 8 to 10 minutes.

2. Add the tomatoes, breaking up the whole tomatoes with the back of a spoon. Simmer gently until the sauce thickens, about 10 minutes.

3. Make four little indentations in the sauce with the back of a spoon. Gently break the eggs and carefully fill each indentation with an egg. Use a fork to swirl the egg whites slightly into the sauce (without breaking the yolks). Simmer gently until the egg whites are set, about 10 minutes.

4. Remove from the heat and sprinkle with cilantro.

5. Serve immediately in the skillet with bread of choice.

ELEMENTAL WAFFLES

The four elements are air, water, fire, and earth. They rule our everyday lives without us having to think about it. To represent these forces, either separate the waffles by each elemental ingredient, or layer all five elements atop the waffle for a complete experience.

Makes eight 6-inch (15 cm) waffles

INGREDIENTS

1 cup (120 g) whole wheat flour

1 cup (120 g) all-purpose flour

1 tablespoon baking powder

¼ teaspoon salt

1 teaspoon ground cinnamon for Spirit

2 large eggs

4 tablespoons unsalted butter, melted

1¾ cups (425 ml) buttermilk

Pecans for Air

Blackberries for Water

Apricots for Fire

Chocolate hazelnut spread for Earth

TO PREPARE

1. Preheat a waffle maker on medium-high heat.

2. Whisk together the flours, baking powder, salt, and cinnamon in a large bowl.

3. Whisk together the eggs, butter, and buttermilk in a medium bowl until combined.

4. Pour the wet ingredients into the dry ingredients and whisk until no large lumps remain.

5. Pour a heaping ⅓ cup (53 g) of batter into the waffle maker and close the lid. Cook until golden brown and crisp, 4 to 5 minutes. Repeat with the remaining batter.

6. Keep the waffles warm in a 200°F (95°C) oven.

7. When ready, top each waffle with the corresponding elemental food.

MAGIC HOUR MILK

Each day shortly after sunrise or before sunset a magical time occurs in which daylight is the softest. In this golden hour set your intentions or find your calm center. Give thanks.

Serves 2

INGREDIENTS

2 cups (480g) milk (or a milk substitute like almond milk or coconut milk)

1½ teaspoons ground turmeric

½ teaspoon ground ginger

1 tablespoon coconut oil

Pinch of black pepper

TO PREPARE

1. Put the ingredients in a saucepan over medium heat and stir. When the mixture begins to simmer, remove it from the heat.

2. Pour the liquid into your favorite mug and enjoy while warm.

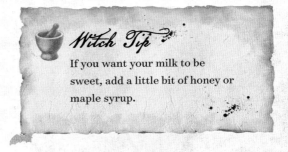

Witch Tip

If you want your milk to be sweet, add a little bit of honey or maple syrup.

Dish Bliss

LUNCH AND DINNER

ENCHANTED FOREST TACOS

There's nothing like walking into Nature and seeing the beauty she has to offer. Tall trees, leafy flora, and some surprising colors. With these tacos, you will create a mini-forest within the tortillas. They will take you there but in the form of delicious breaded cauliflower and ravishing red shredded cabbage!

Serves 4

INGREDIENTS

BREADED CAULIFLOWER

¾ cup (90 g) brown rice flour

¾ cup (180 ml) plain unsweetened almond milk

2 teaspoons garlic powder

2 teaspoons paprika

1 cup (100 g) panko breadcrumbs

1 teaspoon sea salt

1 medium head cauliflower, cut into small florets

1 cup (240 ml) habanero pineapple BBQ sauce or another favorite

2 tablespoons (30 ml) sriracha

LIME CREMA

½ cup (120 g) plain coconut Greek yogurt

2 tablespoons (30 ml) freshly squeezed lime juice

TACO ASSEMBLY

8 corn tortillas

1 cup (110 g) shredded red cabbage

1 avocado, thinly sliced

1 jalapeño, sliced (optional)

TO PREPARE

1. Preheat the oven to 350°F (180°C). Line a baking sheet with parchment paper.

2. To make the breaded cauliflower, in a large bowl, whisk together the flour, milk, ¼ cup (60 ml) water, garlic powder, and paprika.

3. Pour the panko into a shallow bowl or plate and season with the salt.

4. Dip the florets into the batter, making sure they are completely coated. Then roll them in the panko. Lay the coated cauliflower on the prepared baking sheet.

5. Transfer the baking sheet to the oven and bake for 25 minutes.

6. Remove from the oven. In a bowl, stir together the BBQ sauce and sriracha. Dip the florets into the BBQ sauce mixture. Put them back on the baking sheet. Bake for another 25 minutes.

7. While they are baking, make the lime crema. In a small bowl, whisk together the coconut Greek yogurt and lime juice. Set aside.

8. Warm the tortillas. To serve, top each tortilla with the crispy cauliflower, some red cabbage, sliced avocado, some jalapeño (if using), and a drizzle of the crema.

PROTECTIVE BASIL TOMATO SALAD

Basil is an incredible herb that has many uses. In this spell, it's for protection from confusion and fear. With the tomato's powers of love, think of the Universe sending you a gift of nourishment, safety, and clarity.

Serves 4

INGREDIENTS

1½ cups (90 g) fresh basil leaves, plus a sprig for garnish

Olive oil spray

½ teaspoon kosher salt

4 heirloom tomatoes, different colors

2 cups (300 g) 1-inch (2.5 cm) cubes baby seedless watermelon

2 tablespoons (30 ml) extra virgin olive oil

1½ tablespoons (23 ml) good-quality aged balsamic vinegar

1 teaspoon Maldon sea salt

¾ teaspoon freshly ground black pepper

TO PREPARE

1. Preheat the oven to 325°F (170°C). Line a baking sheet with parchment paper.

2. Arrange the basil leaves on the prepared baking sheet. Whisper to the leaves what you need clarity about or protection from. This will enchant them. Mist the sheet with olive oil spray and sprinkle with the kosher salt. Toss to coat and make sure they are in a single layer.

3. Transfer to the oven and bake for 5 to 10 minutes. Check after 5 minutes. They should be dark brown and crispy. Remove from the oven and allow to cool.

4. Wash the tomatoes, core them, and cut them into slices. Arrange on a large platter. As you do so, focus on the love the Universe is sending you. Let it overcome you.

5. Add the watermelon cubes to the platter.

6. Drizzle with the olive oil and balsamic vinegar and season with the Maldon sea salt and pepper. Garnish with a sprig of fresh basil, then sprinkle with the crispy basil leaves.

Witch Tip

Basil is associated with Candlemas, February 1 or 2, so feel free to celebrate with this salad as the world wakes up from its slumber to welcome in Spring.

INTUITIVE PURPLE POTATO SALAD

In witchcraft, the color purple is most associated the third eye chakra, i.e., your psychic abilities like intuition. Your intuition is the guiding light that tells you what you know in your heart to be true. Potatoes promote image magic and enhance spiritual awareness. When you're in need of clarity, this seemingly simple salad will help you open your eyes, all three of them.

Serves 8

INGREDIENTS

2 pounds (910 g) new purple potatoes, cut into 1-inch (2.5 cm) pieces

2 tablespoons (30 ml) avocado oil

1 teaspoon sea salt

1 teaspoon paprika

½ teaspoon freshly ground black pepper

2 shallots, thinly sliced

⅓ cup (80 ml) apple cider vinegar

3 tablespoons (33 g) Dijon mustard

3 tablespoons (12 g) chopped fresh parsley

½ cup (120 ml) extra virgin olive oil

TO PREPARE

1. Preheat the oven to 400°F (200°C). Line a baking sheet with parchment.

2. In a large bowl, combine the potatoes, avocado oil, salt, paprika, and pepper. To enhance your intuition, mix the ingredients with your hands. Toss to evenly coat. Spread in a single layer on the prepared baking sheet.

3. Transfer to the oven and roast until tender and golden brown, 25 to 30 minutes. Let cool for 15 minutes.

4. In a large bowl, combine the shallots, vinegar, Dijon, and parsley. Whisk to combine and then slowly drizzle in the olive oil, whisking until incorporated.

5. When the potatoes are partially cool, toss them into the vinaigrette. Serve warm or at room temperature.

Witch Tip

Have amethyst handy to intensify the salad's magical properties.

POWER BURRITO

In today's fast-paced world, it can be difficult to find time to slow down and focus on what we need. This dish, using the magic of the cilantro chutney to ground you, will channel your energy. With the power of the red onions in this dish, you will feel accomplished in your meal and more present overall.

Serves 4

INGREDIENTS

PICKLED ONIONS

2 cups (320 g) thinly sliced red onion

1 cup (240 ml) red wine vinegar

¼ cup (50 g) raw cane sugar

1 teaspoon sea salt

1 teaspoon whole coriander seeds

1 teaspoon whole cumin seeds

1 teaspoon whole black peppercorns

CILANTRO CHUTNEY

½ cup (120 g) almond or cashew yogurt

¼ cup (60 ml) freshly squeezed lemon juice

1 bunch cilantro, leaves and tender stems

1 cup (48 g) fresh mint leaves

1 jalapeño, roughly chopped

2 teaspoons freshly grated ginger

1 clove garlic

½ teaspoon sea salt

½ teaspoon raw cane sugar

CURRIED POTATOES

2 cups (280 g) peeled and roughly chopped russet potatoes

2 cloves garlic, minced

1 tablespoon (15 ml) coconut oil

1 teaspoon sea salt

2 tablespoons (16 g) curry powder

ROASTED VEGETABLE FILLING

3 cups (300 g) cauliflower florets

One 14-ounce (392 g) can chickpeas, rinsed and drained well

2 tablespoons (30 ml) avocado oil

1 teaspoon sea salt

1 tablespoon (8 g) ground coriander

1 tablespoon (8 g) ground cumin

½ teaspoon crushed red pepper flakes

1 teaspoon whole coriander seeds

1 teaspoon whole fennel seeds

BURRITO ASSEMBLY

4 large tortillas

2 cups (60 g) baby spinach

TO PREPARE

1. To make the pickled onions, combine the onion, vinegar, sugar, salt, coriander, cumin, and peppercorns in a medium saucepan over medium-high heat. Bring to a boil, decrease the heat to low, and simmer for 2 minutes. Remove from the heat. The onions can be made up to 1 week ahead of time and stored in an airtight container in the fridge.

2. To make the cilantro chutney, combine the yogurt, lemon juice, cilantro, mint, jalapeño, ginger, garlic, salt, sugar, and 1 tablespoon (15 ml) water in a high-powered blender. Blend until smooth and creamy. The chutney can be made up to 1 week ahead of time and stored in an airtight container in the fridge.

3. Preheat the oven to 425°F (220°C). Line a baking sheet with parchment paper.

4. To make the potatoes, add the potatoes to a large pot and cover them with water. Bring to a boil over high heat, decrease the heat to medium, and cook until tender, 15 to 20 minutes.

5. While the potatoes are cooking, make the filling. Spread the cauliflower and chickpeas in a single layer on the prepared baking sheet. Drizzle with the avocado oil. Season with the salt, ground coriander, cumin, red pepper flakes, coriander seeds, and fennel seeds. Transfer to the oven and roast for 20 minutes, or until the cauliflower is tender and browned, stirring halfway through the cooking.

6. Once the potatoes are tender, drain them, reserving 1 cup (240 ml) of the cooking water. Add them back to the pan along with the reserved water, garlic, coconut oil, salt, and curry powder. Mash until combined and slightly chunky.

7. When ready to assemble, lay the tortillas out on a flat surface. Smear one-fourth of the potato mixture in the center of each tortilla, and top with ½ cup (15 g) of the spinach and one-fourth of the roasted vegetable filling. Fold the top and bottom in and roll the sides over to form a burrito.

8. Heat a large griddle over medium heat. Add the burritos and crisp on both sides, until browned and crispy, about 4 minutes per side.

9. To serve, cut each burrito in half and serve with the chutney and pickled onions.

TYPHON'S BLACK SERPENT RAMEN

Typhon is one of the deadliest Greek mythological monsters. He's a half-man, half-serpent creature, who has black snakes comprising his lower half. Like all monsters, he's a powerful force to be reckoned with. As you craft this ramen, imagine yourself tackling this powerful beast as a stand-in for whatever forces are in your way.

Serves 4

INGREDIENTS

8 cups (1.9 L) filtered water

4 kombu seaweed squares

One 3-inch (7.5 cm) piece fresh ginger, roughly chopped

4 cloves garlic, smashed

½ cup (30 g) shiitake mushroom stems

¾ cup (180 g) white miso

10 ounces (280 g) dried black-rice ramen noodles, cooked according to package directions, drained, and reserved

4 teaspoons (20 ml) toasted sesame oil, divided

1 cup (70 g) fresh shiitake mushrooms, stems removed and sliced

4 baby bok choy, stems removed and washed

2 large carrots, peeled and thinly sliced

1 cup (120 g) snow peas, strings removed

1 cup (140 g) fresh peas

TO PREPARE

1. In a large stockpot over high heat, add the water, kombu, ginger, garlic, and mushroom stems. Bring to a boil, reduce the heat to a simmer, and cook until flavorful and reduced by half, about 3 hours.

2. Strain the broth and discard the solids. Return the broth to the stockpot. Whisk in the miso. The broth can be made up to this point, cooled, and frozen for later use. If using right away, cover and keep warm.

3. Divide the noodles among bowls. In a large sauté pan over medium heat, add 1 teaspoon of the oil. When hot, add the mushrooms and sauté until tender, about 3 minutes. Divide the cooked mushrooms among the bowls.

4. In the same sauté pan, add another 1 teaspoon of oil. Once hot, add the baby bok choy and sauté for 2 minutes. Divide among the bowls.

5. In the same sauté pan, add another 1 teaspoon of oil. Once hot, add the carrots and sauté until crisp-tender, about 3 minutes. Divide among the bowls.

6. Lastly, add the remaining 1 teaspoon oil. Once hot, add the snow peas and fresh peas and sauté for 1 minute. Divide among the bowls.

7. To serve, ladle the miso broth over the noodles and vegetables and serve hot.

ROOT CHAKRA CROSTINI

The root chakra is the base chakra. It's our foundation and the place we must start all energy explorations. For our purposes, crostini will act as the root chakra. They can serve as an underpinning for any kitchen spell or recipe.

Makes about 24 crostini

INGREDIENTS

1 baguette (fresh or a little stale)

Olive oil

Kosher salt

Freshly ground black pepper

TO PREPARE

1. Preheat the oven to 350°F (180°C).

2. Cut the baguette into slices ¼ inch (6 mm) thick. Divide the slices between two baking sheets.

3. Brush both sides of the bread slices with the olive oil and sprinkle lightly with the salt and pepper.

4. Bake the crostini until crisp and lightly golden, 12 to 18 minutes.

Witch Tip

For extra association with the base chakra, pair with any red-colored foods.

MULTICHAKRA TAPAS

Chakras are our energy centers. In order, there's the root chakra (red), sacral chakra (orange), solar plexus chakra (yellow), heart chakra (green), throat chakra (blue), third eye chakra (purple), and crown chakra (white). With this recipe, you can call upon the colors of each ingredient to awaken the energies within. You'll notice that the throat chakra, used for speaking your truth, is missing because you'll be too busy enjoying your meal!

Makes 24 tapas (6 of each kind)

INGREDIENTS

1 recipe Root Chakra Crostini (page 43)

1 cup (255 g) ricotta cheese

1 scallion, thinly sliced

RICOTTA, TOMATO, AND PEPITA

1 tomato, quartered and sliced

2 tablespoons pepitas

Pinch of dried oregano

Spread six crostini with ⅓ cup (85 g) of the ricotta. Top each one with the tomato slices, the pepitas, the oregano, and some scallion.

RICOTTA, CUCUMBER, AND LOX

¼ hothouse cucumber, cut thinly into 12 slices

2 ounces (57 g) lox or smoked salmon, cut into small pieces

Fresh dill sprigs

Spread six crostini with ⅓ cup (85 g) of the ricotta. Top with two slices of cucumber, a piece of lox, the dill, and some scallion.

RICOTTA, SALAMI, AND JALAPEÑO

1 large radish, cut thinly into 12 slices

12 thin slices salami

12 slices pickled jalapeño

Spread six crostini with ⅓ cup (85 g) of the ricotta. Top each one with two slices of radish, two slices of salami, two slices of pickled jalapeño, and some scallion.

MANCHEGO, ONION, AND HARISSA

6 small slices Manchego

6 teaspoons harissa

½ small onion, thinly sliced into half-moons

Top six crostini with a slice of Manchego, spoon on 1 teaspoon of the harissa, and top with the onion.

Witch Tip

Drink a blue beverage, such as blueberry lemonade, to have all chakras present.

HALF-MOON SQUASH AND POMEGRANATE SALAD

The Half-Moon phase occurs between the New Moon and the Full Moon. It's a time rife with possibilities. In this salad spell, you will harness the energies of the Half-Moon and use the pomegranate arils to send your petitions up to Mother Moon while she nourishes you in return.

Serves 6

INGREDIENTS

2 delicata squash, cut in half lengthwise, seeds removed, and cut into ½-inch (1.3 cm) half-moons

3 tablespoons (45 ml) extra virgin olive oil, divided

1 tablespoon (15 ml) maple syrup

¾ teaspoon sea salt, divided

¾ teaspoon freshly ground black pepper, divided

½ cup (85 g) quinoa, rinsed

1 cup (240 ml) vegetable broth

1 tablespoon (11 g) Dijon mustard

1 tablespoon (15 ml) maple syrup

¼ cup (60 ml) balsamic vinegar

5 ounces (140 g) purple baby kale

1 cup (140 g) pomegranate arils

¼ cup (35 g) roasted salted pepitas

TO PREPARE

1. Preheat the oven to 400°F (200°C). Line a baking sheet with parchment paper.

2. In a large bowl, toss the squash with 1 tablespoon (15 ml) of the olive oil, the maple syrup, ¼ teaspoon of the salt, and ¼ teaspoon of the pepper. Place on the prepared baking sheet and bake for 18 to 20 minutes, until tender and caramelized. Cool slightly.

3. While the squash is roasting, make the quinoa. In a small saucepan over medium heat, add the quinoa and vegetable broth. Bring to a boil, reduce the heat to a simmer, cover, and cook for 15 minutes. Turn off the heat and allow to cook an additional 5 minutes. Remove from the heat and let cool slightly.

4. In a large salad bowl, combine the mustard, maple syrup, vinegar, remaining ½ teaspoon salt, and remaining ½ teaspoon pepper. Whisk to combine, and then slowly drizzle in the remaining 2 tablespoons (30 ml) olive oil and whisk until incorporated.

5. Add the kale, pomegranate arils, pepitas, cooled squash, and quinoa. Toss to coat in the dressing.

PERSEPHONE'S VEGETABLE BOUNTY

Persephone is the goddess of spring and vegetation. She is the one who makes the flowers and plants grow. This collection of veggies can be used as an offering to her or as a celebration of what she's given you.

Serves 4 to 6 • Use a 14-inch (43 cm) round platter

INGREDIENTS

2 cups (490 g) blue cheese dip or dressing

6 thin rainbow carrots

1 cup (150 g) grape tomatoes

2 cups (120 g) broccoli florets

2 cups (125 g) snap peas

2 cups (230 g) small radishes, halved

6 mini sweet peppers

4 ounces (113 g) green beans, trimmed

2 cups (150 g) cauliflower florets

½ cup (34 g) curly kale or parsley, torn into small pieces, to garnish

TO PREPARE

1. Fill a bowl with the blue cheese dip and place at the center of the platter.

2. Working clockwise from the top, surround the dip with the carrots, tomatoes, broccoli, peas, radishes, sweet peppers, green beans, and cauliflower.

3. Fill in any gaps with the small pieces of kale, and top the dip with another piece.

Witch Tip

You can swap out vegetables here based on your changing moods and different intentions.

BEAN AND BUTTERNUT SQUASH BREW

Being psychic isn't all about crystal balls and dimly lit places. It's about taking care of oneself and enhancing the craft whenever possible. Thankfully, with the mental power–enhancing celery, the prophetic dream–inducing onion, and the psychic power–affirming bay leaf, this brew will incite your innate abilities and fill you up at the same time.

Serves 4

INGREDIENTS

SOUP

2 tablespoons (30 ml) olive oil

1 sweet onion, diced

2 ribs celery, diced

2 carrots, peeled and diced

6 cloves garlic, minced

1 tablespoon (15 g) tomato paste

2 bay leaves

1 teaspoon dried thyme

1 teaspoon dried oregano

½ teaspoon sea salt

1 teaspoon freshly ground black pepper

One 2-pound (910 g) butternut squash, peeled, seeded, and cut into ½-inch (1.3 cm) cubes

One 28-ounce (784 g) can crushed tomatoes

6 cups (1440 ml) vegetable broth

Two 14-ounce (392 g) cans cannellini beans, drained and rinsed

2 cups (60 g) rainbow Swiss chard, cut into ribbons

1 tablespoon (2 g) chopped fresh rosemary

CASHEW PARMESAN

1 cup (140 g) raw cashews

¼ cup (10 g) nutritional yeast

1 teaspoon sea salt

1 teaspoon garlic powder

TO PREPARE

1. To make the soup, heat the olive oil in a large Dutch oven over medium heat. Add the onion, celery, and carrots and cook until softened, about 3 minutes.

2. Stir in the garlic, tomato paste, bay leaves, thyme, oregano, salt, and pepper until fragrant and well combined, about 1 minute. Focus on your specific ability here and take what you need from the herbs as you stir.

3. Add the butternut squash, crushed tomatoes, and vegetable broth and bring the soup to a simmer. Cover, decrease the heat to medium-low, and simmer until the squash is tender, 15 to 20 minutes.

4. Stir in the cannellini beans, Swiss chard, and rosemary and adjust the seasonings. Cook for an additional 5 minutes.

5. While the soup finishes, make the cashew parmesan. In the bowl of a food processor, add the cashews, nutritional yeast, salt, and garlic powder. Blend until it resembles grated parmesan cheese, about 1 minute.

6. Ladle the soup into bowls and top with the cashew parmesan.

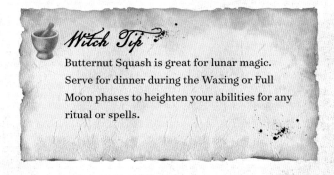

Witch Tip

Butternut Squash is great for lunar magic. Serve for dinner during the Waxing or Full Moon phases to heighten your abilities for any ritual or spells.

SELF-LOVE-STUFFED ACORN SQUASH

For any wand to work or cauldron to bubble, a witch needs to practice self-love. In this spell, the acorn squash, representing personal power, promotes grounding and self-focus. The leeks, apples, and chestnuts all brim with the affection you need to be your authentic witchy self.

Serves 8

INGREDIENTS

SQUASH

4 acorn squash, about 1 pound (455 g) each, halved lengthwise and seeded

1 teaspoon sea salt

½ teaspoon freshly ground black pepper

1 teaspoon olive oil

STUFFING

2 tablespoons (30 g) vegan butter, such as Miyoko's

3 tablespoons (45 ml) olive oil

2 cups (210 g) cleaned and sliced leeks

2 cups (240 g) diced celery

½ cup (120 ml) white wine

1½ cups (225 g) peeled and diced green apple

4 cloves garlic, minced

2 teaspoons minced fresh thyme

½ teaspoon sea salt

½ teaspoon freshly ground black pepper

4 cups (400 g) cubed day-old whole wheat sourdough, crusts removed

1 cup (150 g) cooked chestnuts, roughly chopped

¼ cup (35 g) dried cranberries

½ cup (120 ml) cashew or almond cream

½ cup (120 ml) vegetable broth

TO PREPARE

1. Preheat the oven to 350°F (180°C). Line a baking sheet with parchment paper.

2. To make the squash, sprinkle the flesh sides of the acorn squash with the salt and pepper. Place it cut side down on the prepared baking sheet. Brush the outside with the olive oil. Transfer to the oven and bake until just tender, 25 to 30 minutes.

3. While the squash is roasting, make the stuffing. In a large sauté pan over medium heat, melt the butter with the olive oil. Once hot, add the leeks and celery. Cook, stirring occasionally, until softened, 7 to 8 minutes.

4. Add the white wine and cook until most of the wine has evaporated, 3 to 4 minutes.

5. Add the apples, garlic, and thyme and cook until the apples are just tender, another 5 minutes. Remove from the heat and season with the salt and pepper. Transfer to a large bowl.

6. Add the bread, chestnuts, cranberries, cashew cream, and vegetable broth. Stir well.

7. Once the squash has baked, remove it from the oven and turn it flesh side up. Divide the stuffing among the 8 squash halves and return to the oven. Bake until the stuffing is golden brown, 18 to 20 minutes. Transfer to a platter and serve.

MAGIC MUSHROOM WELLINGTONS WITH RED WINE ELIXIR

Throughout history, mushrooms have been a cause for celebration, a sign that fae are about, and a healing tool for the sick. In magic, they can open our third eye and connect us with the god Neptune. Served with a sweet elixir, this dish will uplift and empower you.

Serves 4

INGREDIENTS

PORTOBELLO MUSHROOMS

4 portobello mushrooms

1 tablespoon (15 ml) olive oil

½ teaspoon sea salt

½ teaspoon freshly ground black pepper

CREMINI MUSHROOMS

1 pound (455 g) cremini mushrooms, wiped clean and quartered

2 tablespoons (30 ml) olive oil

2 shallots, minced

4 cloves garlic, minced

1 tablespoon (3 g) minced fresh thyme leaves

½ teaspoon sea salt

¼ teaspoon freshly ground black pepper

2 tablespoons (30 ml) cashew or almond cream

WELLINGTONS

2 vegan puff pastry sheets

1 tablespoon (15 ml) aquafaba (chickpea water)

1 tablespoon (15 ml) unsweetened cashew or almond milk

1 teaspoon olive oil

½ teaspoon maple syrup

ELIXIR

2 cups (480 ml) fruity red wine, such as Pinot Noir or Beaujolais

1 cup (240 ml) mushroom broth

2 teaspoons date syrup

TO PREPARE

1. Arrange a rack in the middle of the oven and preheat the oven to 425°F (220°C). Line a baking sheet with parchment paper.

2. To make the portobello mushrooms, remove the stems and scrape out the gills with a spoon. Take a moment to appreciate their magical presence. Arrange the mushrooms on the prepared baking sheet and season with the olive oil, salt, and pepper. Transfer to the oven and roast for 12 to 15 minutes. Remove from the oven and allow to cool.

3. Reduce the oven temperature to 400°F (200°C).

4. To make the cremini mushrooms, in the bowl of a food processor, add the cremini mushrooms and pulse until roughly chopped, about 20 pulses.

5. In a large sauté pan over medium heat, add the olive oil. Once hot, add the minced shallots and cook, stirring occasionally, for 2 minutes. Add the garlic and stir.

6. Add the chopped cremini mushrooms and cook, stirring occasionally, until the mushrooms are tender and the moisture has evaporated, 6 to 8 minutes. Season with the thyme, salt, and pepper.

7. Stir in the cashew cream and cook until thick and creamy, another 2 to 3 minutes.

8. To assemble the Wellingtons, cut each sheet of puff pastry into two equal pieces. Roll them out with a rolling pin until they are large enough to wrap your portobello mushrooms inside. Place one roasted portobello mushroom in the center of each puff pastry sheet. Divide the cremini mushroom mixture among the portobello mushrooms. Fold the pastry around the mushrooms, gathering the four points together and squeezing them to seal. Place back onto your parchment-lined baking sheet.

9. In a small bowl, whisk together the aquafaba, nut milk, olive oil, and maple syrup. Brush the pastries with the mixture.

10. Transfer to the oven and bake until the pastry is puffed and golden, 25 to 30 minutes.

11. While the Wellingtons are baking, make the elixir. In a small saucepan over medium heat, add the red wine and broth. Bring to a simmer, reduce the heat to low, and continue to simmer until reduced by half, about 20 minutes. Stir in the date syrup and keep warm until ready to serve.

12. To serve, arrange the Wellingtons on a platter and allow guests to pour the elixir on top.

RED SUN CHILI

A red sunset is one of the most centering and grounding activities you can experience.
Draw your power from this vibrant source to build great foundations in life.

Serves 6

INGREDIENTS

1½ tablespoons olive oil, divided

½ cup (55 g) diced onion

1 large red bell pepper, diced

½ cup (60 g) thinly sliced celery

1 tablespoon minced fresh garlic

1¼ pounds (1.25 kg) 93 percent lean ground turkey

4 teaspoons chili powder

1 tablespoon paprika

1½ teaspoons ground cumin

¼ teaspoon cayenne pepper

One 14.5-ounce (392 g) can fire-roasted diced tomatoes

One 14.5-ounce (392 g) can crushed tomatoes

2 tablespoons tomato paste

1 teaspoon salt

Pinch of ground black pepper

2 fresh bay leaves

¼ cup (15 g) chopped fresh parsley

TO PREPARE

1. Heat 1 tablespoon of the oil in a large pot over medium-high heat. Add the onion, bell pepper, celery, and garlic and cook until they begin to soften, about 3 minutes.

2. Add the remaining ½ tablespoon oil and the ground turkey. Cook until the turkey begins to brown, 3 to 4 minutes. Drain any liquid.

3. Add the chili powder, paprika, cumin, and cayenne pepper and cook until the turkey is no longer pink and the spices are fragrant, 3 to 4 minutes.

4. Add the fire-roasted tomatoes, crushed tomatoes, ½ cup (60 ml) of water, the tomato paste, salt, and black pepper and stir until well combined. Bring the mixture to a boil and stir in the bay leaves. Reduce the heat to medium-low, cover, and simmer for 30 minutes, stirring occasionally.

5. Remove the bay leaves and stir in the parsley. Serve hot.

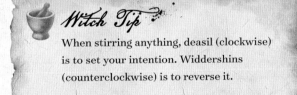

Witch Tip

When stirring anything, deasil (clockwise) is to set your intention. Widdershins (counterclockwise) is to reverse it.

CROW FAMILIAR NESTS

Familiars are complex spirits who can possess living beings like cats, dogs, or crows. These dark-feathered creatures, most associated with death, make excellent familiars due to their intelligent nature and maternal instincts. Make these nests to commemorate your wise winged companion.

Makes 10 nests

INGREDIENTS

8 ounces (227 g) angel-hair pasta

1 cup (245 g) marinara sauce, divided

Freshly grated Parmesan, to garnish

TO PREPARE

1. Preheat the oven to 375°F (190°C).

2. Bring a large pot of water to a boil. Once boiling, salt the water and cook the pasta to al dente, according to the package directions.

3. Drain the pasta and return it to the pot. Toss with half of the sauce.

4. Spray a 12-cup muffin pan or baking sheet with nonstick cooking spray. Using tongs or forks, twist the pasta into nests and transfer to the muffin pan or baking sheet (about ⅓ to ½ cup, or 45 to 70 g, of pasta per nest). Repeat with the remaining pasta to make 10 nests.

5. Fill the nests with the remaining marinara sauce.

6. Bake until the edges start to turn golden and crisp, about 15 minutes.

7. Use a spatula to transfer the nests to the serving board, sprinkle with freshly grated Parmesan, and serve immediately.

FATHER SUN'S VEGGIE HARVEST

All plants, including vegetables, need the Sun in order to thrive. Father Sun's light provides the necessary energy for growth and results. This cornucopian dish is perfect for a day of great accomplishment and recognition of good fortune.

Serves 4 to 6 • Use an 8 × 12-inch (20 × 30 cm) platter

INGREDIENTS

1 recipe Invigorating Mint Sauce (recipe follows)

1 bell pepper, sliced and grilled

1 cup (150 g) grape tomatoes

1 small eggplant, sliced and grilled

1 zucchini, sliced on the diagonal and grilled

4 small carrots, halved lengthwise and grilled

1 small red onion, sliced into rounds and grilled

6 ounces (170 g) button mushrooms, grilled

2 cobs sweet corn, cut into 1-inch (2.5 cm) pieces and grilled

Fresh mint leaves, to garnish

TO PREPARE

1. Fill a bowl with the Invigorating Mint Sauce and place on the platter a little right of the center.

2. Place the pepper slices and most of the grape tomatoes at the top-right corner of the platter. Place the eggplant at the top-left corner. Place the zucchini at the bottom-right corner and the carrots on the diagonal at the bottom left.

3. Surround the bowl of sauce with the onions and mushrooms.

4. Fill in any gaps on the left side with the sweet corn pieces and remaining grape tomatoes.

5. Sprinkle with the fresh mint leaves to garnish.

Witch Tip

Place a sunstone near your plate for a deeper connection with the Sun and a way for him to bless your meal.

INVIGORATING MINT SAUCE

Paired with the vegetables on the previous page, this mint sauce will inspire vitality in you.

Makes 1 cup (215 g)

INGREDIENTS

1 cup (215 g) plain yogurt

¼ cup (6 g) chopped fresh mint leaves

1 small clove garlic, finely grated

2 teaspoons fresh lemon juice

TO PREPARE

Combine all the ingredients in a small bowl and refrigerate until ready to use.

THANKSGIVING LEFTOVERS PANINI

Though witches celebrate the autumnal equinox (a.k.a. Mabon), many do have families who celebrate Thanksgiving, a holiday meant for gratitude, community, and stuffing yourself to the brim. A tenet of witchcraft is no wastefulness, so with this sandwich, you can make use of the morning-after turkey and cranberry sauce.

Makes 4 sandwiches

INGREDIENTS

Softened butter, for the bread

8 slices whole wheat sandwich bread

8 ounces (227 g) sliced leftover turkey

8 tablespoons cranberry sauce

6 ounces (170 g) brie, sliced ¼ inch (6 mm) thick

1 cup (20 g) baby spinach

TO PREPARE

1. Preheat a panini griddle to medium-high or a large skillet over medium heat. Lightly butter one side of each slice of bread.

2. Place four of the slices buttered side down on a work surface. Top with a thin layer of turkey, spread with cranberry sauce, then top with brie slices and baby spinach. Place the remaining slices of bread on top, buttered sides facing outward.

3. Working in batches, transfer the sandwiches to the panini griddle or skillet. If using a panini griddle, cook until golden and melty, about 3 minutes. If using a skillet, cook about 3 minutes per side, or until golden and melty.

4. Cut the sandwiches in half, stack on the serving board, and serve immediately.

Witch Tip

If you'd like to make this during Mabon, add some corn, pumpkin, or squash to honor the sabbat.

SIMPLE SUNDOWN PICNIC

Who doesn't love a picnic? And who doesn't love it during sundown? Dusk is the sweet spot between a sunny day and a starry night. As witches, we constantly exist in transitionary periods, so why not take a moment to enjoy it with an assortment of food and a fellow witch, or two.

Serves 4 to 6 • Use a 10 × 18-inch (25 × 45 cm) tray

INGREDIENTS

½ cup (170 g) honey

½ cup (125 g) ricotta

1 cup (120 g) Kalamata olives

Olive oil, to drizzle

1 bunch seedless red grapes

1 Bosc pear, halved

12 thin breadsticks

One 7-ounce (198 g) round Brie, with half cut into wedges

½ cup (135 g) Brazil nuts

1 cup (130 g) dried apricots

1 cup (120 g) green olives

One 3-ounce (85 g) wedge Stilton or other blue cheese

3 ounces (85 g) orange cheddar cheese, sliced

½ cup (65 g) raw cashews

6 ounces (170 g) extra-sharp white cheddar cheese, sliced

½ cup (70 g) almonds

1 cup (150 g) dates

1 baguette, to serve

TO PREPARE

1. Fill bowls with the honey, ricotta, and Kalamata olives. Add a honey dipper to the honey bowl and drizzle the ricotta with olive oil. Place the honey and ricotta bowls near the top right of the tray and the olives near the bottom left.

2. Place the grapes in the top-left corner of the tray and the pear halves in the top right. Lay the breadsticks on the diagonal below the bowl of ricotta, resting them on the rim of the tray.

3. Place the Brie in the center of the tray. Moving in a widdershins (counterclockwise) direction from the top of the Brie, surround it with the Brazil nuts, apricots, green olives, Stilton, orange cheddar, cashews, and white cheddar.

4. Fill the bottom-left corner with the almonds and the bottom-right corner with the dates.

5. Serve with the baguette placed alongside the board.

Enchanting Small Bites

APPETIZERS AND SIDES

TOADSTOOL TOPPERS

Often found nestled in enchanted forests among the magickal moss-lined groves, mushrooms emit powerful auras and can enhance your powers of intuition and provide a deep connection to the fae and gnome folk—the fungus attracts them!

Makes 30 stuffed toppers

INGREDIENTS

30 button mushrooms

8-ounce (227 g) package cream cheese, at room temperature

1 cup (115 g) packed shredded smoked cheddar cheese

1 roasted red bell pepper, chopped

2 scallions, finely chopped

1 clove garlic, crushed

¼ teaspoon kosher salt

¼ teaspoon freshly ground black pepper

Microgreens, to garnish

TO PREPARE

1. Preheat the oven to 375°F (190°C). Remove the mushroom stems and brush off any dirt. Place the mushroom tops gill sides up in a 9 × 13-inch (23 × 33 cm) baking dish.

2. Mix the cream cheese in a large bowl until there are no lumps. Add the smoked cheddar, red pepper, scallions, garlic, salt, and black pepper, and gently mix to combine.

3. Spoon the mixture into the mushroom caps, packing to fill them.

4. Bake until puffed and golden, 25 to 30 minutes.

5. Transfer to your chosen serving platter, sprinkle with microgreens, and serve immediately.

Witch Tip

A simple way to bring Nature's magic into your kitchen is by tapping into the miracles that are fresh herbs. They add flavor to food, scents to bouquets, magic to intentions, and substance to spellwork.

SWEET POTATO HAY PILES

On a chilly autumn day, witches and nonwitches alike gather for a hayride and journey along farmland. These sweet potato piles, infused with image magic, will take you back to those simple times.

Serves 4

INGREDIENTS

2 medium sweet potatoes, about 2 pounds (910 g) total, peeled

1 russet potato, peeled

1 sweet onion

1 teaspoon sea salt

½ teaspoon freshly ground black pepper

3 tablespoons (24 g) potato starch

1½ teaspoons chickpea flour

¼ cup (60 ml) grapeseed oil

¼ cup (12 g) minced chives

TO PREPARE

1. Using the fine shredding attachment on the food processor, shred the sweet potatoes, russet potato, and onion. Transfer to a large bowl.

2. Use paper towels or a clean dish towel to squeeze some of the excess water from the potatoes. Discard the water.

3. Add the salt, pepper, potato starch, and chickpea flour to the potatoes and mix well.

4. Heat the oil in a cast-iron skillet over medium heat. Once hot, add ¼ cup (60 g) or a generous spoonful of the potato mixture to the oil and press down to flatten.

5. Cook for 3 to 5 minutes per side. If the potatoes start to brown too quickly, turn down the heat a little.

6. Drain on paper towels and then transfer to a platter. Sprinkle with the chives and serve hot or at room temperature.

LOVE VITALITY POTION

Sought out through the ages, love potions are some of the most desired spells. They're meant to attract the interest of your beloved, but this potion works a little differently. Instead of attracting love, it's an offer of love to another. And the red ingredients, served in alchemy test tubes or beakers, will give the recipient a new sense of verve.

Serves 4

INGREDIENTS

1 cup (240 g) frozen dragon fruit

1 cup (240 g) frozen strawberries

1 cup (240 g) frozen raspberries

½ cup (120 g) frozen cherries

1 beet, peeled and chopped

½ cup (70 g) pomegranate arils

1 tablespoon (15 ml) rose water

TO PREPARE

1. Add all the ingredients along with 2 cups (480 ml) of water to a high-powered blender. Blend on high speed until smooth and creamy.

2. Serve in test tubes or beakers for the full effect.

YULETIDE WREATH

It's the most wonderful time of the year. Yule is a time for feasting, drinking, and decorations. For this spell, you can do all three. With a few magic touches, you can turn the traditional wreath into something you can eat and be merry about.

Serves 4 to 8 • Use a large round platter

INGREDIENTS

1 yellow summer squash, peeled into ribbons with a vegetable peeler

4 slices black pepper turkey breast

1 cup (150 g) mixed-color cherry tomatoes

10 bocconcini (mini mozzarella balls)

1 red bell pepper, cut into 1-inch (2.5 cm) pieces

1 whole pickle, cut into chunks

1 cup (120 g) pitted green and black olives

18 large slices pepperoni or hard salami

3 mini saucisson

Curly kale, to garnish

Fresh rosemary sprigs, to garnish

Fresh mint sprigs, to garnish

TO PREPARE

1. Thread all the ingredients onto cocktail sticks or skewers, alternating the placement of ingredients on each cocktail stick. For the meat, fold the slices in half and then in half again before threading onto the sticks. For the squash, create waves by folding the ribbons back and forth on each other before threading onto the sticks.

2. To assemble the wreath, place the cocktail sticks in a circle on the platter. Tuck the kale and rosemary into the gaps to fill out the wreath. Add the sprigs of mint on top.

Witch Tip

Pair the wreath with apple cider or wine to have a full-fledged Yuletide meal.

WISH UPON OSTARA FOOD BOARD

Ostara is a time of fertility and possibility. It's when you can hope and dream knowing you have a good shot for your wishes to come true. Each ingredient is infused with fertile magic to make this holiday especially magical.

Serves 4 to 6 • Use a 12-inch (30 cm) square board

INGREDIENTS

1 recipe Flourishing Green Hummus (page 76)

6 ounces (170 g) beet hummus (store-bought or homemade)

10 long flatbread crackers

4 radishes, halved

1 Persian cucumber, sliced on the diagonal

1 cup (53 g) Goldfish crackers

1 large handful snap-pea crisps

1 large handful mini breadsticks

12 pita chips

4 flaxseed crackers

1 cup (90 g) mini pretzels

Fresh herbs, to garnish

TO PREPARE

1. Place the green and beet hummuses in bowls and place at the center of the board, diagonal from each other.

2. Prop up the long flatbread crackers in between the bowls.

3. Place the radishes and cucumber slices at the upper left of the board above the bowls. Fill in the upper-left corner with the Goldfish crackers.

4. Place the snap-pea crisps at the bottom-right corner of the board and fill the bottom-left corner with the mini breadsticks.

5. Place the pita chips at the top-right corner.

6. Fill in any gaps with the flaxseed crackers and pretzels.

7. Garnish with the fresh herbs.

FLOURISHING GREEN HUMMUS

A perfect addition to the Wish Upon Ostara Food Board (page 75), this hummus will give you an extra dose of luscious green power for whatever your Ostara wish could be.

Makes 1⅔ cups (410 g)

INGREDIENTS

1 can (15.5 ounces, or 439 g) chickpeas, drained and rinsed

1 clove garlic, finely chopped

3 tablespoons tahini

1 cup (135 g) frozen peas, thawed

¼ cup (4 g) fresh cilantro leaves

2 tablespoons fresh lemon juice

½ teaspoon kosher salt

2 tablespoons olive oil

TO PREPARE

1. Place all the ingredients in a food processor and pulse until smooth.

2. Store any leftovers in an airtight container in the refrigerator for up to 3 days.

PEACEFUL WATERMELON PIZZA

True to its namesake element, watermelon works with emotions to bring about peace and balance. The bananas and berries combined inspire prosperity, protection, and good fortune. Give to a friend in need or make one to share.

Serves 6

INGREDIENTS

6 watermelon wedges, cut 1½ inches (4 cm) thick

¾ cup (175 g) plain Greek yogurt

1 small banana, sliced

⅓ cup (50 g) raspberries

⅓ cup (50 g) blackberries

Fresh mint leaves and honey, to garnish

TO PREPARE

1. Top each watermelon wedge with a dollop of yogurt (about 2 tablespoons).

2. Top the yogurt with the bananas, raspberries, and blackberries.

3. Garnish with fresh mint leaves and honey. Serve immediately.

DARK MOON FIGS AND BERRIES

The Dark Moon phase of the Moon's cycle is a time of rest and stillness. It's the in-between period before the Moon starts her ascent into Motherhood. So it's the perfect time to recoup and feast on scrumptious figs and berries.

Serves 4 • Use two 8 to 9-inch (20 to 23 cm) dark plates

INGREDIENTS

6 ounces (170 g) Gorgonzola cheese

8 ounces (227 g) Parmesan

9 figs

16 small crackers

1 pound (453 g) black seedless grapes

7 plums

1 cup (145 g) blackberries

TO PREPARE

1. If using, place the Gorgonzola and Parmesan cheeses just right of center on each plate.

2. Cut three of the figs in half and leave the rest whole. Divide the figs between the two plates.

3. If using, lean the crackers upright and shingle them against the sides of the cheeses.

4. Place a small bunch of grapes on each plate.

5. Cut three of the plums in half and leave the rest whole. Divide the plums between the two plates.

6. Fill in any gaps with the blackberries.

Witch Tip

Light black and white candles to symbolize the current Moon phase with the black candle, and welcome in the next with the white candle.

CHROMATIC LUGHNASADH MEZZE

Also known as Lammas, Lughnasadh is the first harvest of the year. So many different types of food have grown and ripened and are there for the taking, transforming gardens into rainbows. Share your colorful creation with friends and loved ones during this special time.

Serves 4 to 6 • Use a 16-inch (40 cm) round platter

INGREDIENTS

2 tablespoons mixed peppercorns, divided

¼ cup (60 ml) olive oil

8 ounces (227 g) hummus

Pinch of paprika

1 cup (240 g) chickpeas, drained and rinsed

1 cup (200 g) tzatziki

3 large radishes, very thinly sliced

1 cup (26 g) tortilla chips

½ red bell pepper, seeded and cut into sticks

¼ hothouse cucumber, cut into sticks

1 medium carrot, peeled and cut into sticks

1 cup (120 g) Kalamata olives

1 cup (120 g) green olives

2 heirloom tomatoes, cut into wedges

½ cup (35 g) shredded red cabbage

Fresh herbs, to garnish

1 lemon, thinly sliced, to serve

Pita bread, to serve

TO PREPARE

1. Crush the peppercorns with a mortar and pestle or in a food processor or spice grinder. Combine the olive oil with 1 teaspoon of the lightly crushed peppercorns in a shallow bowl. Spoon the hummus into a bowl, drizzle with some of the olive oil mixture, and dust with paprika. Top with a few chickpeas and place in the center of the platter.

2. Spoon the tzatziki into a second bowl and drizzle with more of the olive oil mixture. Set to the side of the platter.

3. Moving in a clockwise direction, starting from the top, surround the hummus with the radishes, tortilla chips, peppers, cucumbers, carrots, olives, tomatoes, remaining chickpeas, and cabbage.

4. Sprinkle everything with the fresh herbs.

5. Serve with the remaining olive oil and crushed peppercorns, lemon slices, and pita bread.

Spellbinding Sweets

DESSERTS

AIRY SPRINGTIME PUDDING

Ahh, Spring, a season of youthfulness and joy. The main ingredients in this concoction—coconut, rice, and mango—are governed by Spring's ruler, the element Air. As an element, Air can be light and provide tranquility. This treat, which combines Air's and Spring's forces, will gently blow you away.

Serves 6

INGREDIENTS

1½ cups (240 g) black rice

Two 14-ounce (392 g) cans unsweetened light coconut milk

½ teaspoon sea salt, plus more as needed

½ cup (100 g) organic cane sugar or coconut sugar

½ vanilla bean, split and seeds scraped and discarded

1 cup (240 ml) nut milk

1 lime, juiced, divided

2 ripe mangoes, diced

TO PREPARE

1. Mix the rice, coconut milk, salt, sugar, and vanilla bean in a large pot. Bring to a boil. Reduce the heat to low and simmer, stirring clockwise—to ensure success—occasionally, until the mixture reaches the desired thickness and the rice is tender, about 1 hour.

2. During the last half hour of cooking, add the nut milk and stir more frequently to prevent scorching, as the pudding will absorb most of the liquid. Remove from the heat and add lime juice to taste, reserving the rest for the mango.

3. Taste for salt and adjust as desired.

4. Let cool and serve with diced mango tossed with the remaining lime juice to taste.

BAD VIBES-BANISHING BLUEBERRY COFFEE CAKE

Many adults drink coffee every day to help them wake up. But what many don't know is coffee also banishes negative thoughts or forces within. With this dessert, you will receive not only the magical qualities of the coffee but fierce protection from the blueberries.

Serves 12

INGREDIENTS

Coconut oil spray

1 cup (120 g) all-purpose flour

½ cup (60 g) oat flour

6 tablespoons (75 g) coconut brown sugar

2 teaspoons baking powder

½ teaspoon kosher salt

½ teaspoon ground cinnamon

6 tablespoons (90 ml) aquafaba (chickpea water), lightly whipped

⅓ cup (80 g) unsweetened applesauce

½ cup (120 ml) unsweetened almond or cashew milk

1 teaspoon vanilla extract

1 cup (150 g) fresh blueberries

TOPPING

⅓ cup (40 g) oat flour

3 tablespoons (36 g) coconut brown sugar

½ teaspoon ground cinnamon

¼ cup (60 ml) coconut oil

⅓ cup (45 g) walnuts, chopped

TO PREPARE

1. Preheat the oven to 350°F (180°C). Spray a 9 × 9-inch (23 × 23 cm) baking pan with coconut oil.

2. In a large bowl, whisk together the flour, oat flour, coconut sugar, baking powder, salt, and cinnamon.

3. In a medium bowl, whisk together the aquafaba, applesauce, milk, and vanilla.

4. Add the wet ingredients to the dry ingredients and whisk until just incorporated. Do not overmix. Fold in the blueberries.

5. Pour the batter into the prepared pan.

6. To make the topping, in a small bowl, combine the oat flour, brown sugar, cinnamon, oil, and walnuts. Mix until crumbly.

7. Scatter the mixture over the top of the batter. Transfer to the oven and bake until a toothpick inserted in the center comes out clean, 25 to 30 minutes.

8. Serve warm.

ILLUMINATING LEMON POPPY CIRCLETS

Lemons and poppy seeds are commonly combined for their taste, but there's also an unfamiliar magical reason. Lemon carries the ability for one to experience spiritual opening within oneself. Poppy seeds provide heightened awareness. Together, they increase our clarity and certainty, allowing the practitioner a glimpse into the light.

Makes 12

INGREDIENTS

DOUGHNUTS

Coconut oil spray

2¼ cups (270 g) oat flour

½ cup (60 g) finely ground almond flour

1 tablespoon (6 g) poppy seeds

1 teaspoon baking soda

½ teaspoon baking powder

¼ teaspoon kosher salt

½ cup plus 2 tablespoons (150 ml) warm water

½ cup (120 ml) unsweetened almond milk, at room temperature

2 tablespoons (30 ml) freshly squeezed lemon juice

2 tablespoons (12 g) lemon zest

3 tablespoons (45 ml) coconut oil, melted

¼ cup (50 g) coconut sugar

¼ cup (60 ml) maple syrup

1 teaspoon vanilla extract

GLAZES

½ cup (60 g) organic powdered sugar, divided

1½ teaspoons lemon juice

1 teaspoon unsweetened almond milk

1 teaspoon poppy seeds

Witch Tip

To add some intention to the recipe, notice the shape of the doughnuts. As you're making the circlets, think about how spiritual awareness is a circle of learning and growing.

TO PREPARE

1. Preheat the oven to 350°F (180°C). Spray two doughnut pans with coconut oil.

2. To make the doughnuts, in a large bowl, whisk together the oat flour, almond flour, poppy seeds, baking soda, baking powder, and salt.

3. In a medium bowl, whisk together the water, milk, lemon juice, lemon zest, coconut oil, coconut sugar, maple syrup, and vanilla.

4. Add the wet ingredients to the dry and whisk until just incorporated. Do not overmix.

5. Divide the batter between the prepared doughnut pans. Tap the pans to release any air bubbles. Transfer to the oven and bake until a toothpick inserted near the center comes out clean, 10 to 14 minutes.

6. Allow to cool on a rack for 10 minutes. Tap the pans on a flat surface to loosen the doughnuts and then flip the pan upside down to release them. Allow to cool completely on the wire rack.

7. While the doughnuts are cooling, make the glazes. In a small bowl, combine ¼ cup (30 g) of the powdered sugar and lemon juice. Whisk until combined. In another small bowl, whisk together the remaining ¼ cup (30 g) powdered sugar, almond milk, and poppy seeds.

8. Dip the doughnuts in the lemon glaze and then drizzle with the poppy glaze. Transfer back to the wire rack to allow the glaze to firm up.

PLANET JUPITER CHEESECAKE

Jupiter is the fifth planet in our solar system and is ruled by the god of the same name. As a strong planetary force, Jupiter has made its mark on Earth with pumpkins, which we will be using here. With this spell, you can harness Jupiter's nurturing power.

Serves 16

INGREDIENTS

CRUST

¾ cup (150 g) raw cane sugar or coconut sugar

1 teaspoon ground cinnamon

8 sheets phyllo dough, thawed

1 cup (240 ml) coconut oil, melted

FILLING

½ cup (70 g) raw cashews, soaked in water for 2 to 8 hours, drained, and rinsed

¼ cup (60 g) mashed ripe banana

One 14-ounce (392 g) package silken tofu

½ cup (100 g) coconut sugar

⅓ cup (65 g) brown coconut sugar

3 tablespoons (45 ml) coconut oil, melted

2 tablespoons (16 g) cornstarch

2 tablespoons (30 ml) freshly squeezed lemon juice

1 tablespoon (15 ml) vanilla extract

½ teaspoon grated orange zest

¼ teaspoon sea salt

1¼ cups (300 g) canned pumpkin puree

1 teaspoon ground cinnamon

½ teaspoon ground ginger

¼ teaspoon ground nutmeg

TO PREPARE

1. Preheat the oven to 400°F (200°C). Line a baking sheet with foil. Have a 9-inch (23 cm) springform pan ready.

2. To make the crust, in a small bowl, combine the sugar and cinnamon.

3. Brush one sheet of phyllo dough with the melted coconut oil (as you work, keep the remaining phyllo dough covered with a damp kitchen towel) and sprinkle with some of the sugar mixture.

4. Starting at one short end, fold the phyllo in half over the coconut oil mixture and brush with more coconut oil. Transfer to the springform pan, oil side down, gently pressing into the bottom and sides.

5. Repeat with the remaining 7 sheets of phyllo, the coconut oil, and the sugar mixture, arranging in overlapping layers to completely and evenly cover the bottom and sides of the pan.

6. Place on the prepared baking sheet to catch any drippings. Transfer to the oven and bake for 15 to 20 minutes or until crisp and golden. Let cool while you make the filling.

7. Decrease the oven temperature to 350°F (180°C).

8. To make the filling, in a high-powered blender, combine the drained and rinsed cashews, banana, tofu, coconut sugar, brown sugar, coconut oil, cornstarch, lemon juice, vanilla, zest, and salt. Blend until smooth and creamy, about 1 minute. Add the pumpkin and spices and blend until smooth.

9. Pour into the prepared crust and transfer to the oven. Bake for 45 to 50 minutes. The cheesecake will be done when the top is lightly puffed and the edges are golden. Remove from the oven and allow to cool for 20 minutes. Transfer to the refrigerator and chill for 4 hours or up to overnight.

10. To serve, remove the springform, dip a knife in ice water, and slice.

Witch Tip

Decorate your altar with violet, rich purple, blue, or yellow flatware or fabrics in honor of the giant planet.

KARMA CARROT CAKE

The idea of karma is cause and effect. When we do good, good things come back to us. And those deeds ripple outward. With the healing properties of carrots and the good intentions of the kitchen witch, this confection can be given as an olive branch or simply a nice gesture for someone else.

Serves 16

INGREDIENTS

CAKE

Coconut oil spray

1¼ cups (300 g) unsweetened applesauce

2 cups (400 g) coconut sugar

9 tablespoons (135 ml) aquafaba (chickpea water)

1 cup (120 g) all-purpose flour

1 cup (120 g) finely ground almond flour

1½ teaspoons baking powder

1 teaspoon baking soda

½ teaspoon kosher salt

1 teaspoon ground cinnamon

2 cups (240 g) freshly grated carrot

1 cup (100 g) shredded unsweetened coconut

1 cup (240 g) crushed pineapple in juice, do not drain

FROSTING

½ cup (120 g) vegan butter, such as Miyoko's, at room temperature

8 ounces (225 g) vegan cream cheese, at room temperature

1 teaspoon vanilla extract

3 cups (360 g) organic powdered sugar

TOPPING (OPTIONAL)

1 cup (140 g) toasted, chopped pistachios

1 cup (100 g) toasted sweetened shredded coconut

TO PREPARE

1. Preheat the oven to 350°F (180°C). Line two 9-inch (23 cm) cake pans with parchment paper and spray with coconut oil.

2. To make the cake, in a large bowl, combine the applesauce, coconut sugar, and aquafaba. Whisk to blend.

3. In another large bowl, whisk together the all-purpose flour, almond flour, baking powder, baking soda, salt, and cinnamon. Add the dry ingredients to the wet ingredients and stir to combine.

4. Add the carrots, coconut, and crushed pineapple to the mixture and stir until just combined. Divide the mixture between the prepared pans and transfer to the oven. Bake until a toothpick inserted in the center comes out clean, 35 to 40 minutes.

5. Let the cakes cool for 10 minutes before removing from the pans and cooling completely on a wire rack.

6. While the cakes are baking, make the frosting. In a large bowl with a handheld mixer or in the bowl of a stand mixer, combine the softened butter and cream cheese. Whisk on medium speed until combined. Add the vanilla.

7. Slowly incorporate the powdered sugar until the frosting is smooth and creamy.

8. To frost the cake, invert one layer on a cake stand or platter. Spread half the frosting over the first layer. Add the other layer on top and spread the other half of the frosting over it. Add the toasted pistachios and/or coconut, if desired. Refrigerate for at least 1 hour prior to serving.

FELICITY ORANGE ISLAND PIE

As a magical fruit, oranges bring about blessings and happiness. Much like an island getaway. Retreat with your little slice of sweet, enchanted paradise.

Serves 8

INGREDIENTS

CRUST

1 cup (140 g) raw almonds

½ cup (70 g) pecans

3 Medjool dates, pitted

¼ teaspoon sea salt

FILLING

2 cups (280 g) raw cashews, soaked for at least 4 hours, drained, and rinsed

⅓ cup (80 ml) maple syrup

½ cup (120 ml) coconut oil

3 tablespoons (18 g) grated orange zest

⅓ cup (80 ml) freshly squeezed orange juice

1½ teaspoons vanilla extract

WHIPPED COCONUT CREAM

One 14-ounce (392 g) can full-fat coconut milk, refrigerated overnight

1 tablespoon (15 ml) vanilla extract

2 teaspoons maple syrup

TO PREPARE

1. Line a 7-inch (18 cm) springform pan with parchment paper.

2. To make the crust, add the almonds, pecans, dates, and sea salt to the bowl of a food processor. Process until a sticky dough forms. Add a splash of water if needed to bring it all together.

3. Press the crust into the prepared pan, making sure you bring it about 1 inch (2.5 cm) up the sides of the pan.

4. To make the filling, add the soaked and rinsed cashews, maple syrup, coconut oil, orange zest, orange juice, and vanilla to a high-powered blender. Blend until smooth and creamy.

5. Pour into the springform pan and smooth with a spatula.

6. Cover and transfer to the freezer for at least 3 hours.

7. While the pie is freezing, make the whipped cream. Start by placing a mixing bowl in the freezer for 10 minutes.

8. Once your bowl is cold, remove the can of cold coconut milk from the refrigerator. Carefully remove the top of the can; do not shake or tip upside down. Scoop the thick layer of coconut cream from the top of the can, leaving the water at the bottom for another use.

9. Using a whisk attachment, beat the coconut cream on medium speed until the cream becomes light and fluffy and peaks form, 2 to 4 minutes. Add the vanilla and maple syrup and beat until just incorporated.

10. When ready to serve, pipe dollops of the whipped cream onto the pie and enjoy!

Witch Tip

Serve on a blue plate to get the full effect and to promote tranquility.

DIVINE PATIENCE WHITE PEACH AND FIG GRANITA

With kitchen witchery, patience truly is a virtue. Like any other spell, it takes time to get the desired results. Thankfully, fig has the property of divination, and peaches inspire wisdom. Though this granita has many steps, they will give you the necessary discipline to complete the spell.

Serves 6

INGREDIENTS

½ cup (100 g) coconut sugar

5 ripe white peaches, pitted and chopped

5 fresh ripe figs, chopped

TO PREPARE

1. In a medium saucepan over medium heat, combine 2 cups (480 ml) water and the sugar and stir until the sugar is dissolved, about 5 minutes. Set aside to cool.

2. In the bowl of a food processor, add the peaches and figs and process until smooth.

3. Add the pureed fruit to the cooled sugar mixture and stir to combine.

4. Pour the mixture into an 8 × 8-inch (20 × 20 cm) metal baking dish and place in the freezer for 1 hour.

5. After 1 hour, remove the baking dish from the freezer and, using a fork, rake the top of the granita. Transfer back to the freezer and freeze for another hour. Repeat every hour for 4 hours, or until the mixture has a snow-like texture.

ATTRACTING STORGÊ PEAR TARTE TATIN

Storgê is the love between family or friends who feel like family. It's a warm and sometimes complicated form of love. If you want to bring your dear ones close, the pear will facilitate that sweet affection.

Serves 8

INGREDIENTS

½ cup (100 g) coconut sugar

3 tablespoons (45 g) vegan butter, such as Miyoko's

2 tablespoons (30 ml) freshly squeezed lemon juice

4 Anjou or Bartlett pears, ripe but firm

1 vegan puff pastry sheet, thawed

1 recipe Whipped Coconut Cream (page 98; optional)

Witch Tip

Serve during Mabon or Yule for an extra cozy dessert.

TO PREPARE

1. Preheat the oven to 375°F (190°C).

2. In a 10-inch (25 cm) cast-iron skillet, stir together the sugar and 2 tablespoons (30 ml) water. Cook over medium heat, without stirring, until the mixture turns golden brown, about 5 minutes. Stir in the butter. Stir in the lemon juice.

3. While the sugar mixture is cooking, peel the pears, cut in half, and remove the cores.

4. When the caramel is ready, arrange the pear halves in concentric circles. Turn the heat to medium-low and cook until the pears are tender, 3 to 4 minutes.

5. Lay the puff pastry sheet out on a clean, dry surface. Cut the pastry into a circle slightly bigger than the pan you are using, about 11 inches (28 cm). Prick the pastry randomly with a fork. Place the pastry over the top of the pears, tucking the overlap into the pan.

6. Transfer to the oven and bake until the pastry is puffed and golden, 25 to 30 minutes.

7. Place the pan on a wire rack and allow to cool for 15 minutes.

8. Run a knife around the edges of the skillet. Place a serving platter on top of the pan, and carefully invert the tart onto the platter. Allow to cool for 5 minutes longer and then serve warm with whipped coconut cream if desired.

MIDNIGHT BERRY PAVLOVAS

We know midnight to be the witching hour, but it can also be the perfect time to put on the cauldron and brew up these light-as-a-specter meringue confections.

Makes 10 to 16 mini pavlovas

INGREDIENTS

MERINGUES

4 large egg whites

1 teaspoon cream of tartar

1 cup (200 g) caster sugar

1 teaspoon pure vanilla extract

½ cup (75 g) blueberries, to garnish

½ cup (75 g) blackberries, to garnish

Confectioners' sugar, to garnish

WHIPPED CREAM

1 cup (235 ml) heavy whipping cream

1 teaspoon pure vanilla extract

2–4 tablespoons confectioners' sugar (alter per desired sweetness)

TO PREPARE

1. To make the meringues: Preheat the oven to 225°F (105°C). Line two baking sheets with parchment paper and set aside.

2. In a very clean bowl of a stand mixer with the whisk attachment, beat together the egg whites and cream of tartar at medium speed until frothy like shaving foam. Increase the speed to high and add the sugar gradually, 1 tablespoon at a time, beating until you have stiff and glossy peaks. Reduce the mixer speed to low and add the vanilla.

3. Transfer half of the mixture to a large piping bag fitted with a large closed-star tip (such as Wilton 1M). Pipe the meringues into 2- to 3-inch (5 to 7.5 cm) nests and slightly indent the centers with the back of a spoon. Repeat with the remaining meringue mixture.

4. Bake for 1 hour 15 minutes, until the meringue no longer feels tacky to the touch, then turn off the oven and cook for 30 more minutes, or until the oven is cool. Meringues can be stored at room temperature in a dry place for 3 to 5 days.

5. When ready to serve, make the whipped cream: Add the heavy whipping cream to a bowl of a stand mixer. Beat the cream until just stiff, reduce the speed and add in the vanilla extract and amount of confectioners' sugar of your choosing. Beat until fully combined.

6. Transfer the mixture to a clean 18-inch (46 cm) piping bag, fitted with the same closed-star piping tip used for the meringues, and pipe a rosette on top of each meringue.

7. Place blueberries and blackberries in the center of each rosette and dust with confectioners' sugar just before serving.

CHEESECAKE SPELL JARS

There's nothing quite like whipping up a spell in the cauldron and then having it tucked away in a jar. Glass jars are perfect for herb mixtures, brews, and especially cheesy confections.

Makes 6 jars

INGREDIENTS

12 ounces (340 g) cream cheese, at room temperature

3 tablespoons sugar

1 cup (235 ml) heavy cream

1 tablespoon fresh lemon juice

¼ cup (85 g) dulce de leche

2 tablespoons slivered almonds

½ teaspoon Maldon sea salt

¼ cup (85 g) chocolate fudge sauce

2 tablespoons mini chocolate chips

3 tablespoons honey, plus more to drizzle

1 cup (125 g) small raspberries

TO PREPARE

1. Using a handheld mixer, beat together the cream cheese and sugar in a large bowl until smooth.

2. On low speed, gradually add the heavy cream. Increase the speed to high and beat until thick and stiff, about 2 minutes. Beat in the lemon juice.

3. Divide the batter among six 7- to 8-ounce (205 to 235 ml) squat bulb or tulip jars. Refrigerate for 2 hours.

4. To serve, spoon the dulce de leche over two of the jars and sprinkle with the almonds and sea salt. Spoon the chocolate fudge sauce over two of the jars and sprinkle with the chocolate chips. Spoon the honey over the two remaining jars and top with the raspberries, open sides down, and drizzle with additional honey.

VENUS VALENTINE OFFERING

Valentine's Day is a day for celebrating love and basking in sugary treats. For matters of love, Venus is one of the reigning goddesses. This Valentine's Day make a platter for Venus to thank her for what she's given and for what you're yet to receive.

Serves 6 to 8 • Use a 12-inch (30 cm) oval platter

INGREDIENTS

1 to 2 handfuls conversation hearts candies

4 pieces chocolate of your choice

3 heart-shaped gumdrops

6 small heart-shaped sugar cookies

3 Linzer cookies

7 chocolate-drizzled strawberries

3 frosted heart-shaped cookies

4 white chocolate–covered pretzels

1 chocolate-covered heart-shaped donut

4 mini heart-shaped sugar cookies

TO PREPARE

1. Fill a heart-shaped bowl with the conversation hearts and place at the center of the platter. Place the chocolate above the bowl and the heart-shaped gumdrops below it.

2. Moving in a clockwise direction from the top right of the platter, fill the perimeter with three small sugar cookies, the Linzer cookies, four chocolate-drizzled strawberries, the frosted heart cookies, the white chocolate–covered pretzels, the remaining sugar cookies, the remaining chocolate-drizzled strawberries, and the donut.

3. Fill in any gaps with the remaining heart cookies.

SPOOKY SAMHAIN TREATS

Samhain, a.k.a. Halloween, is all about the creepy and scary. Though for most witches it's a day of communing with the dead, there's always room for a little bit of magical fun. Call on your familiars, don your capes, and wield your wands. This day belongs to the night.

Serves 6 to 8 • Use an 8 × 12-inch (20 × 30 cm) tray

INGREDIENTS

1 cup (200 g) candy corn

12 to 16 foil-covered chocolate eyeballs

½ cup (6 g) caramel popcorn

1 cup (200 g) pumpkin candy corn

½ cup (89 g) gummy worms

3 spooky pretzel fingers and 3 chocolate sprinkle dipped pretzel rods

12 to 16 strawberry licorice twists

2 eyeball gummies

2 vampire gummies

¼ cup (28 g) mini pretzels

2 ghost lollipops

TO PREPARE

1. Fill a decorative pumpkin bowl with the candy corn and place in the bottom-right corner of the tray. Fill a bowl with the foil-covered eyeballs and place in the top left. Fill another bowl with the caramel popcorn and place in the center of the tray.

2. Place the pumpkin candy corn directly in the tray below the bowl of eyeballs and the gummy worms to the right of the bowl of eyeballs.

3. Place three "finger" dipped pretzel rods in the top-right corner and three chocolate sprinkle dipped pretzel rods in the bottom-left corner. Place the licorice twists above the chocolate sprinkle pretzel rods.

4. Fill in the gaps with the gummy eyeballs, vampire gummies, mini pretzels, and ghost pops.

CAREER-BOOSTING PECAN SPHERES

Whether you're starting a new career or trying to maintain good performance in your current job, these pecan spheres can help. Pecans are associated with employment and success. They can give you the boost you need to make a great impression. And you don't even need your cauldron to make them!

Serves 8

INGREDIENTS

1 cup (140 g) organic pecans

8 Medjool dates, pitted

1 teaspoon vanilla bean powder

½ teaspoon sea salt

½ cup whole sesame seeds

½ cup whole black sesame seeds

TO PREPARE

1. Combine all the ingredients except the sesame seeds in the bowl of a food processor. Process until the mixture is roughly chopped and pulls away from the bowl in a sticky ball.

2. Scooping out teaspoons at a time, squeeze the mixture between your palms and roll into a tight ball.

3. Place the sesame seeds and black sesame seeds in separate shallow bowls. Roll half of the pecan spheres in the sesame seeds and the second half in the black sesame seeds until you get full coverage.

4. Place in an airtight container and transfer to the refrigerator. Chill for 30 minutes before enjoying.

Witch Tip

Take these spheres with you to empower you in your workspace, and perhaps share some with your coworkers!

CAULDRON OF NOURISHMENT

Your hearth serves as command central for nourishing yourself, your spirit, your intentions, and everything you hold dear. It also contains all the vital mystical elements for prosperity and health: wood, fire, earth, metal, and water.

To keep your magical practice open and well tended, reach for your trusty cauldron to concoct this blessed stew. While no real recipe exists, add what you have, call on your kitchen spirits for what you need, and your family will be sustained no end.

A dash of basil for great courage when rocky roads prevail.

A frond of dill, a sprig of mint——keep safe along life's trail.

A pinch of sage for in those times when wisdom it does fail,

And yarrow leaves to heal what hurts and comfort what does ail.

Some cinnamon, when sprinkled on, smells sweetly of success,

With lavender and chamomile for sleep and peaceful rest.

So, stir and sip and add a dash of salt for flavor's sake——

My wish for you, a seasoned life, is there for you to take.

INDEX

First published in 2022 by Rock Point, an imprint of The Quarto Group,
142 West 36th Street, 4th Floor, New York, NY 10018, USA
T (212) 779-4972 F (212) 779-6058 www.Quarto.com

Contains content previously published in 2020 as *The Plant-Based Cookbook*, *The Complete Guide to Self Care*, and *House Magic*, and in 2021 as *Fabulous Food Boards* by Chartwell Books and Wellfleet Press, imprints of The Quarto Group, 142 West 36th Street, 4th Floor, New York, NY 10018, USA.

Rock Point titles are also available at discount for retail, wholesale, promotional, and bulk purchase. For details, contact the Special Sales Manager by email at specialsales@quarto.com or by mail at The Quarto Group, Attn: Special Sales Manager, 100 Cummings Center Suite 265D, Beverly, MA 01915 USA.

10 9 8 7 6 5 4

ISBN: 978-1-63106-912-3

Library of Congress Control Number: 2022932858

Publisher: Rage Kindelsperger
Creative Director: Laura Drew
Managing Editor: Cara Donaldson
Cover and Interior Design: Laura Klynstra
Editorial Assistants: Katelynn Abraham and Makiah Stephens

Printed in China

This book provides general culinary information. However, it should not be relied upon as recommending or promoting any specific diagnosis or method of treatment for a particular condition, and it is not intended as a substitute for medical advice or for direct diagnosis and treatment of a medical condition by a qualified physician. Readers who have questions about a particular condition, possible treatments for that condition, or possible reactions from the condition or its treatment should consult a physician or other qualified healthcare professional.

For entertainment and educational purposes only. Do not attempt any spell, recipe, procedure, or prescription in this book otherwise. The author, publisher, packager, manufacturer, distributor, and their collective agents waive all liability for the reader's use or application of any of the text herein. Use great caution when working with fire by having plenty of water or a fire extinguisher at the ready.

The Quarto Group denounces any and all forms of hate, discrimination, and oppression and does not condone the use of its products in any practices aimed at harming or demeaning any group or individual.